Advice From
A Patient

Advice From A Patient

Insights from Those Who Needed
Care for Those Who Provide Care

HALEY SCOTT DEMARIA
and DIANE S. HOPKINS

Hardcover ISBN: 978-1-64704-005-5

Published in the United States by Bublish, Inc.

Contents

Dedications

I am pleased to dedicate this book to my mother, Patricia Serbin, who was an exceptional caregiver for three girls, her husband and her mother. ~ Diane

I dedicate this book to my first caregivers, my parents, Stephen and Charlotte Scott, who have always given me the most compassionate care; and to my children, James and Edward, for whom I hope I have done the same. ~ Haley

Acknowledgements

When I first met Diane Stover Hopkins, I was inspired by her energy to improve the healthcare experience for patients. Having been a long-term patient myself, I was keenly aware of the importance of compassionate care. I am grateful to Diane for her drive and her willingness to include me in her mission to elevate the patient experience for all patients.

Thank you to the medical professionals who have made a difference in my life: Dr. Steven Garfin, Dr. Eric Zeidman, Dr. Roger Klauer; and nurses: Debbie Vinson, Laura from ICU, and those who cared for me when I was unaware.

And most importantly, thank you to my husband, Jamie, who never waivers in his patience and understanding. I am grateful for his support in everything I do. He is changing lives in the healthcare field himself, so it's fun to share a little bit professionally with him.

- Haley

First, I need to acknowledge my dear friend Haley who ignited new ideas for me when I first met her and heard of her dramatic medical story and her ongoing accomplishments. I'm honored to know you Haley and thankful we've combined forces to impact care whenever we can!

Thanks also to dear friends and family who have shared their views and stories generously and who have been great supporters of wild and crazy ideas! Thanks to my son Benjamin, husband Robert, my sisters Jodi and Carol; and my wonderful woman crew including: Tinker, Franni, Diane, Sharon, Beth, Elaine, Carol, Teri, Gaylene, Cindy, Karen, Lauren, Lara, Corina, Danielle, Sally, Deb, Erin, Lori, Sue, Maggie and Rosie.

-Diane

And of course, sincere thanks to the wonderful people who generously shared their stories and perspectives with us for this book!

"Begin to see the patient gown as a cloak of respect that represents a season of suffering for a human being. When we are in this season of suffering, we take on the gown of a patient. No one would wear one of these outfits if they weren't already diminished by illness. The patient gown must become a signal to all that there is a patient in need... a wounded person...a fellow human in need of special respect."

-Erie Chapman

Introduction

O ur paths came together when Haley was willing to share her story of triumph over injury and her book, **What Though The Odds** with the staff at Memorial Health System in South Bend where Diane was the Chief Marketing Officer. Our first meeting sparked years of collaboration and more shared stories from our mutual medical encounters. Due to our shared passion for elevating the patient experience, and the ongoing need for enhancements, this book became a logical next step in our work to raise awareness and engagement.

We have combined our own perspectives with those of some remarkable contributors who enthusiastically agreed to share their advice for the industry. This compilation of stories is designed as a reminder for the busy and wonderful caregivers who juggle so many priorities beyond their patients every day.

A patient survey offers a snapshot of satisfaction and comments, but it does not always allow for thoughtful, detailed recommendations. We trust this fresh look at the voice of the patient and their families will illustrate the perspectives of what is important to those compromised by illness or injury.

Of course, not all advice is relevant to all situations, but hopefully the intentions around exceptional caring will be relevant to all who read this book!

Let's keep the Care in Healthcare!

Diane and Haley

The Best Possible Use of This Book...

For those training healthcare professionals:

This book can complement the facts, figures, procedures, and policies that novice clinicians must understand before progressing to their licensure and careers of caring. The stories from real patient experiences can be a balance to the science as new professionals begin to establish their approaches to care.

For existing caregivers:

Despite lengthy training, years of dedication and commitment, it is very easy to be distracted by the demands of important healthcare work, and to forget for a minute or a month, the needs, desires, fears, and hopes of individual patients. This book serves as a solid reminder to reduce the risk of complacency and insensitivity.

For patients or future patients:

This book offers constructive guidance, affirmation, and appreciation for one of the most complicated professions and industries: healthcare. Some of the concepts and stories shared will help patients to navigate their own medical journeys. Others stories will offer a sense of community through common experiences. Overall, this book was developed with the belief that sharing is caring!

Haley's Journey as an Expert Patient: Miracles and Advice

I had a relatively healthy childhood. Doctors were for well-visits and vaccinations, with one hiccup in the form of stitches in my knee (thanks to the zipper on a suitcase…don't ask). However, as a freshman swimmer at the University of Notre Dame in South Bend, Indiana, our team was in a bus accident. Two of my teammates were killed; I was left paralyzed and told I would never walk (or swim) again. After 20 months, five surgeries, 100s of hours of physical therapy, and several months in the hospital, I competed again for the Fighting Irish. Two years later, I would have my sixth and final back operation.

I used to joke with my mom that – after everything I had been through - I should be given an honorary medical degree. Of course, I was not a medical expert; but I did find myself in a position of being an expert in patient care. Throughout my recovery, I spent time in three different hospitals: a small regional medical center; a large level-one trauma center; and a small, private "fancy" hospital in Southern California. Each hospital had its unique culture and its unique level of care.

When we are in the thick of a medical emergency, a frightening diagnosis, or just a routine appointment, all we know is what we experience. We trust our medical *professionals – as we should. But there are times when our care varies: when care is exceptional, but also when compassion is checked at the door. And, as patients, we are often so consumed with our medical issues that when compassion is lacking, we do not have the energy or frame of reference to know any differently.*

That needs to change.

When I first connected with Diane, we shared the same belief that compassion is most important during our most vulnerable times. She had the administrative background, and I had the story. Together we present our experiences in a way that engages the hearts and minds of those who can make a difference in the day-to-day lives of all patients.

Diane's Patient Experience Journey: Sharing Advice

I *have been blessed to have had minimal medical issues throughout my life. As I built a career in healthcare administration, a time came when my dear father, Frank Serbin was diagnosed with vascular dementia. Although that was tragic news, the good news was that I had moved back to the Philadelphia area to be close to my parents in 2013 and had the honor to spend 2 years caring for him. This first-hand view of healthcare through a new lens, improved my ability to better understand why thoughtful patient experience strategies are crucial for the industry.*

In 2006, I was working to re-invent patient experience strategy for Memorial Hospital of South Bend. Having worked in the industry for many years, I had seen many fads come and go, and our team decided some innovative approaches were needed.

One strategy that rose to the top of this work was how crucial it is for hospital staff to be engaged with their hearts and minds. Traditionally, patient satisfaction efforts revolved around monitoring and sharing survey scores: numbers that indicated how well we were doing. But the facts didn't always lead to improved performance. I also realized that 90% of hospital workers desired to do the very best for their patients, but due to many distractions and conflicting priorities, they some-times forgot who they were serving and how best to serve. Thus, my belief that medical professionals need "reminder strategies" to engage the heart and the head in order to have a successful improvement movement.

This discovery led to the first of a variety of heart/ head efforts. As a new way to reach staff, I wrote the poem, ADVICE FROM A PATIENT, to illustrate sustainable patient-centered behaviors. The intention was that we share it with hospital leaders and all staff members. The poem was very well received within the organization and helped boost exciting new commitments to the work. Hospitals around the country requested use of the poem, which I was happy to share.

Below is a copy of the FIRST ATTEMPT that planted the seeds for this book:

Advice from a Patient
written by Diane S. Hopkins

This may be a normal day at work for
you, but it's a big day in my life.

The look on your face and the tone of your voice
can change my entire view of the world.

Remember, I'm not usually this needy or scared.

I'm here because I trust you, help me stay confident.

I may look like I'm out of it, but I
can hear your conversations.

I'm not used to being naked around
strangers. Keep that in mind.

I'm impatient because I want to get the
heck out of here. Nothing personal.

I don't speak your language well. You're
going to do what to my what?

I may only be here for four days, but I will
remember you the rest of my life.

Your patients need your patience.

Reprinted with permission. Memorial Health System

"In the sick room, ten cents' worth of human understanding equals ten dollars' worth of medical science."

— Martin H. Fischer

"Never doubt that a small group of thoughtful committed people can change the world, indeed it is the only thing that ever has."

— Margaret Mead

Advice from Patients and Families

Note: Some contributors chose to remain anonymous, however their passion for sharing their insights with caregivers is sincere.

Our hope is that all caregivers will read this in the spirit of continually learning and improving the systems and approaches for every patient, every shift.

We Need to Rely on You

Advice from Carol Struett

Going through a life-altering diagnosis
can be scary but I found that it eased my
concerns by relying on the staff nurses.

During treatments, when the body is being tested
and your stamina and willpower are at their lowest,
some of the best part of my care was the uplifting
advice and encouragement from my nurses. They
provided emotional support whenever it was
needed. They were always knowledgeable, listened
to every concern and held my hand when needed.

One time, at the peak of my exhaustion and
tears, the nurse grabbed both of my hands
and held them tight. She told me how strong
I was and that I can get through it OK.

Sometimes that's all that is needed
and patients should look for that one
nurse that will be your angel.

Patients… always, always ask questions.

Caregivers…always, always welcome questions.

The Coach Coaches Caregivers

ABILITY is what you're capable of doing.
MOTIVATION determines what you do.
ATTITUDE determines how well you do it.

-Lou Holtz

Trained healthcare professionals have the ABILITY to do their job. Making a difference, or collecting a paycheck, might be the MOTIVIATION to do your job. But your ATTITUDE is all a patient will see, hear, and feel...So make sure you have a good one.

"*Our sorrows and wounds are healed only when we touch them with compassion.*"

— *Buddha*

"*Nobody cares how much you know, until they know how much you care.*"

— *Theodore Roosevelt*

How Dare You?

*"How Dare You," was the last thing we ever thought
we'd need to say, To those who were there giving Dad
care. As we dealt with the shock of his failing health, As
we faced life without him sitting in his favorite chair.*

*"How Dare You," wasn't what we expected to feel,
As we anguished over treatment plans. As his
needs were not met from shift to shift, We also
anguished over leaving him in your hands.*

*As his requests were ignored and he was labeled
unruly, We spent more and more time in his room.
As his nutritional restrictions were missed meal by
meal, We pressed that discharge had to be soon.*

*As conflicting information was so hard to
process, As we struggled to understand what
was right. We often felt lost in the hospital maze,
Instead of partnering we felt we must fight.*

*Thank you for taking the time to read,
Advice from those who count on you. The
Do Know Harm promise that frames your
work, Must be the core of all that you do!*

A compilation from The Serbin Family- Honoring the Life of Frank Serbin

"Care more for the individual patient than for the special features of the disease...Put yourself in his place...The kindly word, the cheerful greeting, the sympathetic look—these the patient understands."

-William Osler

"We are what we repeatedly do. Excellence, therefore, is not an act, but a habit."

-Aristotle

As I Age

A Letter for my future Doctors and Nurses

I'll end up spending much more time with you all
As I age.

I'll need more drugs and assistance
when I'm with you

As I age.

My eyes may deceive me, my stride will be slower
so I'll need more of your guidance and patience

As I age.

My memory may be a bit slower and my needs
for food faster but I'll try to be a good patient

As I age.

Please remember I'm a little different
and I'll depend more on your knowledge,
empathy and strength as I try to hold onto
my dignity, my well-being and my life

As I age.

Baring Yourself as a Part of Critical Caring

By Melinda, Texas

I was in an auto-pedestrian accident on May 19, 2014. I was the pedestrian. I suffered a subarachnoid hemorrhage and other injuries. I was in ICU and step-down ICU for 9 days.

I received excellent care, and have one experience with a nurse, that truly stands out. I had a large open wound at my hairline and lost a small chunk of my scalp. On day 7, I was finally allowed to shower (with my wound covered) and wash my long thick crusty blood filled hair, I was ecstatic! Then, I found out that I would not be allowed to shower on my own because I could fall and sustain another brain bleed. I was mortified at the thought of someone helping me shower - while I was naked! The young nurse started to run the faucet and I started crying. I was so embarrassed and tried to convince her that I could do it myself. I am a trial lawyer, and thought I was being super persuasive. I wasn't. She kept trying to reassure me. I told her I couldn't do it and tried to negotiate just washing my hair in a sink. Denied, due to my TBI. Finally, she kneeled down at my feet and pulled back her long thick black hair, and showed me a huge scar from the base of her neck, along up the side of her head that went nearly to her forehead. She had a brain tumor removed. She said that she knew how I felt because someone had to help bathe her too.

I'd never been more grateful to take a shower, and never been more grateful to a nurse for sharing her vulnerability to help me though one of the most challenging experiences in my life.

Advice: Be ready to bring yourself and your stories to help your patients through things they never thought they'd be facing. Thank you, thank you for trying.

"When a patient codes, the first pulse to check is your own."

— *Dr. James Reinig*

"A healthy attitude is contagious, but don't wait to catch it from others. Be a carrier."

— *Tom Stoppard*

What You All Think
Vs.
What We Patients Need

Many in healthcare believe they've spent so much time preparing their minds and they know what care to provide… but we need you to know us. We need you to know each of us one by one not just diagnosis by diagnosis. We need you to know our need for peace and quiet, for company and sometimes for permission to break down.

We need your information in a way we can understand it.

You may think you need to focus on the medical procedures but we need you to first be a translator for us. We need you to translate the lingo, the directions, the risks, the conflicting information and the abbreviations.

We need to be your full focus for the minutes we're together.

We need the coldness of this healing place to be warmed by how you look us in the eye, how you happily fetch a heated blanket, how you welcome our family to our temporary home away from home and how bright lights are softened.

We need your warmth.

Thank you, Thank you for your Dedication and Care!

"People pay the doctor for his trouble; for his kindness they still remain in his debt."

— *Seneca, 4 BC*

"Success as a therapist is not found in DOING something for the patient, but rather in BEING someone for the patient."

— *Ili Rivera Walter*

Real Advice: Ice Cream for Breakfast

Written by Amy C.

My caregiving journey started decades before my mom passed away when my mom was diagnosed with Parkinson's disease in June 1997. Abandoned after a divorce, and ill, my mom was lonely, depressed, and anxious. The Parkinson's brought many unwelcome side-effects, and with each side effect, it seemed another medication was dispensed to treat the symptoms. The pills never addressed the root causes or dealt with the emotional pain beneath the physical ailments.

Important Advice from my mom's journey?

1. She hated the loss of control over her body and the loss of her independence. Her transition from caregiver to patient changed her behavior.
2. Finding <u>gentle</u> caregivers to spend time with my mom made the biggest impact.
3. The hospice care workers were the best because they worked with compassion. One combed my mom's thinning hair every day in the final weeks of her life. She also gave her sponge baths, dressed her in her favorite t-shirts and painted her nails. It was the best care she received.

4. The MOST important thing to my mom was to be treated as a person…a living, feeling, sensitive being. Patients are frightened, anxious, and in need of touch, love and compassion. The meds, pokes, pills and "cures" are not as meaningful to a dying patient as are the caresses, songs, prayers, soft music and *ice cream for breakfast, lunch and dinner.*

Important advice from a caregiver?

Coordination of care and communication among care providers (doctors, therapists, care givers) was lacking for us and is a crucial part of healthcare.

Please remember to talk to one another to keep care up to date.

Please remember we want to get to the bottom of the situation not just placate symptoms.

Please remember to strive to never leave unanswered questions

Witnessing a loved one endure a chronic illness is emotionally exhausting. While death brings closure to the disease and earthly worries, it also brings a profound sense of loss and grief. Sometimes, systems in place to support and care for the dying lack compassion and empathy, further burdening the loved ones left behind.

Thank you for remembering this.

Embrace Confidence, Not Arrogance

By Haley DeMaria

In the summer between my freshman and sophomore years of college, I needed to have back surgery to straighten the kyphosis in my spine. It was to be a long and complicated surgery. My dad had researched many surgeons, and we initially decided on Dr. G in San Diego.

When we met with Dr. G, he explained the details of the operation and was quite specific and graphic. (So much so, that my cousin had to leave the room because she felt faint. I did not have that option; I had to listen to everything that would happen to me.)

I remember at the end of our meeting, the only thing I could think of to ask was, "And you think you are the best person to do this?"

Dr. G's response was calm, simple, and to the point: "Yes, I am. But you should meet with other surgeons just to make sure."

Me: "But you're the best."

Dr. G: "Yes."

His quiet confidence was comforting. It wasn't arrogant, but he didn't beat around the bush. I was going to be in the best hands possible.

R.N. (Required Nudging)

Nurse Debbie came at night, her 1st task: review my case. 27 years later, I can still see her face

I don't often remember our words, it was late and I wasn't well. But I always knew when Nurse Debbie arrived, All my fears I could tell.

She wasn't very soft-spoken, but her demeanor was always kind. She was usually no-nonsense, and quite often read my mind

I remember her charge: "You have to pee on your own!" She knew how to motivate: "Or I can't send you home."

Night after night, the uncomfortable was made smooth. On the embarrassing topic, of getting my systems to move

These are the realities of an injury of the spine. I was so grateful for knowing, Nurse Debbie was mine!

Nurses can make or break the care we receive. Be present. Meet your patient where they are, while nudging them to go where they need to go. Literally.

Haley Scott DeMaria

Oh, the Stories We'll Tell

To the dear and important medical professionals in this world:

> *Yes, being in the hospital is a serious thing.*
>
> *This is a scary journey and we must trust your judgement.*
>
> *Yes, it's an admission and a hospital stay,*
>
> *But it's also a story we'll tell likely til our dying day!*
>
> *So, your time with us is memory making.*
>
> *The big and little things that happen will be revealed to all who will listen.*
>
> *Remember you will play a major role in the accounts we will share.*

> *And please remember, absolutely the most important fact is that we live to tell the story!*

"A person who feels appreciated will always do more than what is expected."

— Anonymous

Our Healthcare Wishlist

Written by Maggie Long Scroope

First, above all, we WISH we never had to learn about pediatric heart surgery services and that our precious son never had to experience the many layers of interventions, technology and medications as he began a life that was unbelievably short. However, since we did face these unbelievable circumstances, we developed a WISH LIST of what can make the best of an experience we all would rather avoid.

1) **Wishing for A Friend**: *I wish every patient had a nurse (or any care team member) like we had for our son. Someone who became your friend. Who made the unbearable just a little more bearable…Who had your best interest at heart…Who you could tell really did care. In our instance, she is someone we will remember for the rest of our lives.*

2) **Wishing for Acknowledgement of Moment by Moment Urgency**: *By keeping the cafeteria line moving, it shows they know and care that you only have 10 minutes to grab a bite to eat before your loved one is off to their next test. By letting patients onto a crowded elevator before you, you're telling them that you know your meeting can wait – but your loved one going into surgery cannot. By waiting to clean the floors until after a crucial family huddle*

is done with a care team, you're telling them that their profound moment takes precedence over this task at this moment. By keeping the family room stocked with detergent, snacks, games – you're telling a patient's family that you recognize that while you can go home tonight and live your life as normal, they cannot. The people and processes in place need to center around the care of patients and their families. If not, why are you even there?

3) **Wishing for Authentic Empathy**: *Staff who show appropriate emotion make all the difference for families as their emotions run from high to low, hour by hour.*

4) **Wishing/Praying for Private rooms**: *I cannot imagine our experience if we didn't have our own room to feel at home in.*

5) **Wishing for Experts:** *Most consumers can't do weeks of research to determine which physicians or specialists were top in their class or have advanced skills, especially when you didn't expect to need care at all. We wish that hospitals will always take the extra steps to hire or prepare true experts for the best possible outcomes.*

6) **Wishing for Understanding of Our Personal Needs:** *The ability to continue our life 'on the outside' during the hospital stay (access to Wifi, computers, chargers, stamps, a mailbox, food, crossword puzzles and games, quarters, laundry) helps reduce some stress as you try to be the best extended care-giver.*

"A hospital should also have a recovery room adjoining the cashier's office."

— Anonymous

"Always remember that for each patient you see you may be the only person in their life capable of both hearing and holding their pain. If that isn't sacred, I don't know what is."

— Anonymous

In Your Hands

By Carol Houck, Mother of Chase

As parents of young children, we're accustomed to holding our child's hand, keeping them from harm and caring for their needs. We're used to watching what they eat, put in their mouth, who they're with and what they're up to. We search for ways to make them happy and keep them well. With all of that noted, a day came when our 1-year-old son Chase needed more care than we could provide. He needed experts to save his life. This need ramped up suddenly from a bout of asthma that wouldn't be controlled, even though we had done so many times in the past. Starting that day, like many others, we never expected to hear a doctor tell his father and I "we'll do all we can but that we needed to leave the room and let them intubate him, they needed to take control of his breathing." He was so small and always active and happy; how did we get here? It's still a bit surreal twenty years later.

We did as we were told, we relinquished care to the doctors and nurses. Soon our family members were surrounding his bed in an intensive care unit, control and decision-making for him turned over to strangers, albeit well trained doctors, nurses and other hospital staff, but we were in unfamiliar and very scary territory. The hospital staff didn't know him or us, but we were counting on them to bring our boy back healthy and strong. We learned quickly that day that it was necessary to put him and his well-being In Your Hands, watching you monitor and address his changing needs over a 36-hour period with no guarantees. Fortunately our medical team was amazing, and the outcome was great. Chase was successfully weaned from the machine and we are forever grateful to the dedication and knowledge of the doctors and staff. It was so important for us to feel that our loved one was the most important patient despite the fact that we knew the doctors and their team had many patients and were constantly prioritizing their need for attention. Please try to understand the fear and stress families like ours face at times like this, as we believe our caregivers did, even though it's another day at work for you. We're so fortunate you chose your profession, likely with much sacrifice. Keeping us informed of status, even if all remains the same and providing clear explanations is vitally important to a parent's or guardian's success at relinquishing care and letting you do what you must. I would say that when a family member is in a hospital, all of us are In Your hands.

Let Me be your Sweetie Today

from the experiences of Frank Serbin

One of my nurses told me a tale,
She mentioned that authorities said,
That she and her team mates
must use formal names,
I told her that idea should be dead.

Not everyone is perfectly happy to be
Treated like an impersonal disease.
I like feeling like a member of the family,
In fact, it puts me at ease.

I'm trying to forget the real state I'm in,
I'm dealing with fears and dealing with pain
I look for light-heartedness and for some fun.
I love it when endearment is added to my name.

So even though leaders want
formal language in place,
Remember some of us want to feel like friends,
Call me honey, sweetie or buddy anytime,
It provides comfort while I wait for my stay to end!

"I remember when I used to sit on hospital beds and hold people's hands, people used to be shocked because they'd never seen this before. To me it was quite normal."

— Princess Diana

"Everyday focus on your purpose. Remember why you do what you do. We don't get burned out because of what we do. We get burned out because we forget why we do it."

— Jon Gordon

A Moment in Time

As soon as you walked in the room,
we knew life would change.
There were so many things we imagined you'd say,
So many options and fears at play.
Your words were the worst news
while your expression was kind.
We were well prepared by you
for this moment in time.
You deal with these issues most
every day and it shows.
So many choices and information easily flow.
You balance the facts with an empathetic ear.
You will always be someone we
see as a competent dear.
This sad development puts our
entire family in a bind,
Thank you for staying with us
for this moment in time.

Distracted Care

I spent about a week in the Intensive Care Unit at a level-one trauma center. Most patients in the ICU with me were not conscious. There was an operating table in the middle of the room, because seconds existed between life and death.

I had just had a massive, life-threatening, 9-hour surgery, so I was well-medicated, but I was conscious. Among many tubes and cords, I had a drainage tube leaving the right side of my body. Because of a complication during surgery (which would need to be surgically repaired the following week), I was draining about 2-litres of fluid a day, and the drainage container needed to be replaced often. This process was extremely painful for me.

During one of these replacements, the nurse changing the container barely spoke to me. In fact, I don't remember her speaking to me at all. And while I was fairly "out of it," I do recall – very clearly – the conversation she had with another person I could not see.

My nurse had just returned from maternity leave after the birth of her daughter. Her husband was a doctor, so he didn't have much time to spend with their baby girl. It was her first child, so she missed being home with her, but she also was glad to be back at work even though she was really tired. Her doctor husband was on-call that night, but she was going home after her 12-hour shift.

Details. I remember the details of a conversation she was having with someone else, while I lay in pain as she changed my drainage tube.

This was in 1992, and I can still see her next to me. And I still remember how much her attention was not on me, the patient.

To My Physicians, Nurses and Therapists:

Please treat me like you would your own family.
I really hope you love your family.

The
Top 10
To Do List For
Hospital Staff

1 Remember the healthier you are, the better care you'll give.
2 Please get plenty of sleep the night before my surgery.
3 Please make sure you eat lunch before my afternoon therapy.
4 Remember all of those safety rules that protect you and me.
5 Don't suffer in silence if you have more work than you can do.
6 Wash your hands, Wash your hands, Wash your hands.
7 If you aren't sure if you know what I need, please don't guess.
8 If you have bad news to share, give it to me straight.
9 If you have good news to share, let's have a party!
10 Care for you so you can care for me.

Counting On You

Didn't expect to end up in this bed,

Counting on you to look out for me
when I can't look out for myself.

Didn't expect to have life turned upside down,

Counting on you to help me get right side up.

Didn't expect to be just a patient,

Counting on you to remember I'm a person too.

Didn't expect to not sleep for a week,

Counting on you to keep me from
becoming more weak.

Didn't expect to look so unkept,

Counting on you to remember I used to look good.

Didn't expect to feel alone and scared,

Counting on your experience and
knowledge to make all I didn't expect an
unexpectedly positive experience.

"Kind words can be short and easy to speak, but their echoes are truly endless."

— *Mother Teresa*

"Be patient with patients who are not patient."

— *Anonymous*

"I'm not touching that!"

In 2002, when I was pregnant with my first son, my husband and I met with the head of anesthesiology at the hospital where I was to deliver, to discuss the possibility of an epidural and/or pain medications during delivery. The anesthesiologist confirmed that an epidural would be nearly impossible, based on the location of my spinal fusion. However, there were other drugs available to ease the pain.

He told us his wife was pregnant and due around the same time, and to have the hospital call him if he wasn't on call, and he would come help during my labor.

The night my son was born, we arrived at the hospital around 11pm. We told the nurse to call the head of anesthesiology. She refused: it was the middle of the night and he wasn't on call. We tried to explain our situation and the meeting we had had with him, but she still refused.

When the on-call anesthesiologist arrived, he came into my room, took one look at my scar-covered back and said quite emphatically, "I'm not touching that!"

He was quickly whisked out of the room as I heard the words, "You *can not* say that in front of a patient!" It made me panic, when I was already in a heightened emotional state.

Our pleas to call the head of anesthesiology continued to fall on deaf ears, and I ended up delivering my son naturally, with no drugs, and thankfully, healthy.

Advice for the patient: Make sure all orders (formal and informal) are written down.

Advice for the medical professional: Be careful what you say (and now you say it) in front of a patient.

Can't Stand to Leave Her

Our 87-year-old grandmother had four babies, yet never had a hospital admission. She never had a surgery until her gallbladder decided to get her attention. The surgery went very well, but for the first time she needed to heal and experience drugs she's never had. We were certainly concerned about surgery at this age but trusted the surgeon and knew the surgery was not optional. She was a strong person, but her body was weakening. She was nervous about all that was going on. Despite the worries about her healing, eating and sleeping, the biggest worry of all was leaving her there alone all night.

Although we visited every day, there was no way we could sleep by her side all night long. We couldn't stand to leave her there with strangers. We couldn't stand to leave her alone in case her needs were ignored. The two weeks of worrying and wondering if all was well while she recovered without us were hell for all of us.

Our advice for caregivers in all hospitals is that when patients are all alone in your care, do all you can so they feel like they're never alone. Do all you can to move from stranger to trusted guide. And, when you can, do all you can to put the family at ease when they cannot be there.

Thank you for your expertise, your attention to the little things, they are the big things!

Remember the What Ifs...

Patients are unpredictable as you caregivers well know. As you work with us with confidence and competency it's often easy to imagine that all will go as planned. As you determine what we and our family members need while we're in your care, our advice is that you remember a few "What Ifs" as you navigate the policies and procedures:

What if these turn out to be our last days and I won't leave the hospital alive?

What if I live alone and I'm missing my dog or cat?

What if I have no idea how I'm going to pay for all of the uncovered expenses?

What if I'm afraid to tell you all of the symptoms I'm having?

What if my life is complicated and I'll have no visitors?

What if I don't want a private room? I need someone to talk to?

What if I have many food issues and can't eat whatever arrives?

What if I can't exactly remember my medical history?

Thank you for making What If, a regular part of all you do.

"Kindness is the language which the deaf can hear and the blind can see."

— Mark Twain

"It's not how much you do, but how much love you put into the doing that matters."

— Mother Teresa

Protection From the Patient Sometimes Needed

We never knew about how adding in new drugs in the hospital could lead to a full change in personality.

Although Dad was the patient, his reaction to the drugs had him attacking each of us when we visited. The doctor said it was a temporary reaction, but it was a shocking thing for us. The nurses had their hands full with Dad's needs and all he was going through. But, the nurses saw how he was treating his family with anger, aggression, and threats driven by medication impact on his mind. This was not normal. It would have been easier just to tend to the patient; but when Dad started threatening Mom to "take him home that minute," the nurse realized it was important to take care of Mom too.

Shaken by the unexpected attacks in addition to the stress of the hospital stay, Mom was hurting. The nurse stepped in with Dad and told him he needed to stop the attacks, explained why he was feeling that way and warned him that he would have no more visitors if he was going to attack them. She put her arm around Mom and told him how lucky he was to have family nearby but that she needed to feel safe. She walked with Mom out to a waiting area and offered her a beverage. She gave her clear instructions about what to say and do if he did it again and reassured her that leaving was the right thing to do.

She cared for the visitor as if she was the patient. She took control and helped both Mom and Dad better manage the situation. She had the courage to intervene beyond the medical condition. The reaction passed in 2 days.

Please be willing to influence family issues like this whenever you can.

Quiet Comforts and Unintended Discomfort

Note: Lauren Balestier was 11-years-old when her school bus was in an accident that killed a classmate and a teacher. Lauren's injuries included a fractured pelvis, multiple lacerations requiring stitches and staples, and a crushed hand that was thankfully saved but required her to have her left pinky amputated. Lauren spent 5 days in the PICU, and a year in occupational, physical, and intensive hand therapy. In her words:

The first people I saw after the accident were the people in the ambulance. They were comforting, but it was awkward because they had to take my clothes off.

At the hospital, there was a nurse who made me feel extra special when she gave me stuffed animals. She also played music while I got stitches and when I went into surgery. My nurse made me feel very comfortable and safe.

My favorite part about being in the hospital was when my family came to visit and brought me things.

The hand therapists are my favorite people and after everything we are still in touch. They were more than just my doctors they have become my friends.

My advice: Be sensitive, make patients feel special and safe and encourage smiles.

When Lauren was asked what is the one thing she would change about her hospital stay, she responded "not being at a hospital where priests or nuns come into my room to pray with me." Lauren's family is not religious. At an emotional and delicate time in this young girl's life, she was thrust into the foreign world of prayer that left her feeling uncomfortable.

While the intentions were well-meaning, one should check with the family when offering support for children in the hospital.

Taking Time

My admission to a rehabilitation hospital after a never expected stroke was another big surprise, especially when I learned I may be there for 90 days.

I knew I needed to be there, I knew it was my only way back to health, but I felt trapped. My family couldn't be with me every day so loneliness set in quickly. I was the youngest person on the floor and that felt weird.

The most important way the aides and nurses and therapists helped me with all of this strange-ness was that they took the time to really attend to me. I knew they were busy but they took the time to chat with me, learn more about me, to inquire about what was on my mind and what I was hoping for. They took the time to share words to boost my confidence. They took the time to offer me some perks like therapy later in the morning so I could sleep. They took the time to tell me some jokes and share favorite tv show developments.

Taking time to attend to the person over and above the reasons they're in your care is the best care you can give!

"I've learned that people will forget what you said, people will forget what you did, but people will never forget how you made them feel."

— *Maya Angelou*

"The good physician treats the disease; the great physician treats the patient who has the disease."

— *William Osler*

Dear Doctors:

Thank you for going to all those years of school. Thank you for cramming all that information into your head and for learning the new computer systems. Thank you for being smart about the things most people aren't.

Now that I've experienced needing the brain power of 4 physician specialties, I thank you for being willing to translate your years of knowledge building for me and my family in ways we can understand. Some of you even literally drew a picture!

Thanks also for having a caring heart along with the scientific brain that saves lives!

Sometimes You'll Need to Triple Check: Sometimes patients lie

It probably sounds immature I know.

You had bad news for me and lots of unexpected information to share. You had definitions, percentages, care plans and risks I needed to know and options I had to consider quickly.

I must confess I wasn't really listening. I heard words coming out of your mouth and I saw the seriousness in your eyes. I nodded my head and told you I understood…but I lied. You checked if I had any further questions and I said no…but I lied. You probed a second time and summarized my situation and again asked if I was clear. I lied and said yes.

I never intended to lie. I truly didn't want to understand. I didn't want to be clear about this big change in my life. You didn't bargain on patients who lie, but I didn't bargain on cancer ruining the picture of my life.

My best advice is to remember some patients aren't ready to hear what you're saying and Triple Checking that we understand may help!

It Pains Me

Having never had surgery before, I was gearing up for misery after the surgeon cut me open. I read all the what ifs in the pre-op material. I talked to friends and read too much on the internet. I was more and more anxious.

I was scared to death about the opioid risks and planned to tough it out without them. Then surgery day came. Everyone was kind and efficient. I left the surgery center actually feeling no pain with my emergency narcotics in hand. I got home and slept like a baby. I woke up the next morning and felt a dull ache only. I never needed the hard drugs. The actual pain was so manageable for me and for that I'm very grateful.

What really pained me was thinking about the pain. My advice is that all doctors and hospitals offer a few heavy pain drugs, but not assume everyone will need them. I've seen others get dependent after surgery and there's got to be a new way to look at this.

Thank you for re-thinking pain.

"Keep your thoughts positive, because your thoughts become your words.

Keep your words positive, because your words become your behavior.

Keep your behavior positive, because your behavior becomes your habits.

Keep your habits positive, because your habits become your values.

Keep your values positive, because your values become your destiny."

— Mahatma Gandhi

"You treat a disease, you win or you lose. You treat a person, I guarantee you, you'll win, no matter what the outcome."

— Patch Adams

"To make a difference in someone's life, you don't have to be brilliant, rich, beautiful, or perfect. You just have to care."

— Mandy Hale

The Knock on the Door that Delights

By Amy Shields

My son, Sully, spent over five years being treated for Stage IV Neuroblastoma at a Children's Medical Center. Often during his stays, he would request food from a restaurant located in the adjacent adult hospital. Every time I walked into that adult hospital, I noticed I felt down. It just felt sad in there. The ceilings were low, the lights were dim. The hallways were narrow and confusing, and there was a general feeling of sadness. Upon my return to Children's, I would immediately feel better. You would think that a building filled with sick kids would feel sad, but it's actually the opposite. Children's always feels joyful.

While part of the joyful feeling comes from the building itself, it's mostly the people who make a Children's Hospital feel joyful. On any given week there are a multitude of activities: therapy dog parades, dance parties with music therapy, BINGO games broadcast to patients' rooms with prizes delivered to the winners.

On the oncology floor there is always something to look forward to. Hope for Henry, a local non-profit, brings parties: superhero parties, jewelry making parties, author parties, super bowl parties. As soon as you see the balloons that announce their presence, you know it is going to be a good day (especially because there is always pizza and cupcakes at a Hope for Henry party).

The Mason Strong Foundation stocks the "Brave Bin" with toys, and patients get to pick something fun when they have been brave, like having their chemo port accessed or their blood drawn.

On Wednesday nights you can always count on a visit from the EVAN Foundation with their Treats and Treasures cart. Everyone gets to choose one treat (candy) and one treasure (some sort of toy or game). Usually when you are in the hospital a knock on the door signals a nurse ready to take vital signs or administer medicine. It's so uplifting when a knock at the door brings something joyful.

Adult hospitals (and the whole world really) could benefit from a purposeful shot of joy. The fact that more than five years later, Sully loves going to Children's and actually gets upset when he has to leave, is a testament to the fact that the people there are doing something right.

More joy is the key. These purposeful spaces of joy allow happiness to exist in the same place as pain. Even adults could use a smile from the treat cart.

Sully is a 10-year-old boy who has been battling stage-four neuroblastoma for over five years. He is currently cancer-free, overcoming two prior relapses.

When the Child is the Patient, Parents are Patients Too

by Elizabeth

As a healthy 29-year-old former collegiate athlete, I was deemed a "low risk" pregnancy and sailed through the 9 months with relative ease. When given the choice of what hospital I would deliver, my Ob-GYN saw no reason to be concerned about delivering at our local hospital; one that did not have a level 3 NICU. My labor progressed fairly smoothly and at 1:41pm on Sunday, January 16th, 2005, my son entered the world. He was a full-term and healthy appearing baby who scored a 10 on the APGAR test and weighed in at 7'1". 30 minutes later, a nurse heard heart murmur when listening to his chest, and an hour later, he was transferred to another local hospital where the pediatric cardiologist would perform an echocardiogram. Having just given birth, I remained at the hospital where I delivered.

Two hours later, the cardiologist called to tell me that Jackson had a heart condition that would require urgent surgical intervention. Since no hospital nearby had the capacity to offer this type of surgery, I was given a list of hospitals that could meet Jackson's needs, and was told to choose. What? How am I supposed to know?

I asked the cardiologist where he would send his son, and thankfully, he gave me his opinion. But it was a 5-hour drive to this hospital.

The following morning, Jackson was prepared for his transfer to Atlanta by a medical transport airplane. I was discharged, rushed home to quickly pack, and sat on ice-packs in the backseat as my husband drove for the next 5 hours. When we arrived in Atlanta, I received a call to report that Jackson had arrived safely, and that he was getting settled into the CICU at the hospital. While speaking with the nurse, it became clear that I could have traveled with Jackson on the medical transport plane, but that option was not offered to me. No one had ever taken the time to explain that I had a choice to accompany him or not, which left me feeling like a failure as a new mother. Somehow I was already letting him down.

Don't forget about the parents; they are patients too.

The Trust Test

by Erin Bratton

In healthcare there is one very important component to making the patient/physician relationship work: TRUST.

If the patient doesn't fully trust the physician, the relationship isn't fully understood. To do this, physicians have to be compassionate and relatable to the patient's needs.

Throughout my life I have had many physicians who have passed the TRUST test, and others who have not. When I meet a physician, I know in a matter of ten minutes if the provider is the right fit to take care me. It's not only about the physician's knowledge of medicine, it's about **taking the time to talk and listen to your patient**. The medical charts only say so much about the patient; to establish TRUST, a medical professional has to take the time to talk with the patient.

With many of my providers there is open dialogue within the care. As a young patient my providers were always candid about the fact that *my diagnosis would be long term*, and I was always involved in the decision making in my medical care. Providers not only looked at my case as what was medically necessary but looked at the quality of life.

The best doctors create TRUST by treating the person, not the disease or the tumor.

Erin, age 25, has lived for two decades under the care of a physician. Diagnosed with a (AVM) Atervinous Malformation brain tumor at age 4, she has had scores of surgeries.

Assumptions Can Go Wrong

by Haley Scott DeMaria

When I was in the hospital, after two emergency surgeries to relieve pressure on my spinal cord, I was unaware that two of my teammates had died in the accident that shattered my spine. For the first 36 hours, when I asked how my teammates were, the answer I received was, "You are the only one still in the hospital." Each visitor to my room was told that I did not know about the passing of my teammates. I had endured two risky surgeries; "let her have some time to recover first…"

I thought of this sensitivity in a new light when I recently heard the story of an 11-year-old girl who was also in a bus accident. Lauren lost a friend in the accident, and a finger to amputation. When she was in the hospital, still recovering from her own surgery, a nun came in her room to pray with her: "We pray for those who were killed in the accident."

But Lauren didn't know yet that her friend and her teacher had been killed. No one thought to ask first, talk second, and the moment of sensitivity was shattered. At an emotional and delicate time in this young girl's life, she was thrust into a foreign world of daily prayer that left her feeling uncomfortable, especially when her family wasn't in the room. While the intentions were well-meaning, the assumptions weren't clear regarding what the patient knew. The advice is that even well-intended assumptions can cause un-intended suffering.

Help Calm the Emergency Care Storm...

By Claudia Balestier

My daughter was in a bus accident. When I first arrived at the hospital, I remember three things:

- I watched the nurses **calmly, kindly, and gently** tend to my daughter. I was just glad my daughter was alive, and their kindness and care for her helped me stay calm.

- When we met with my daughter's hand surgeon, he was **very specific** about her injuries. Knowing what we were dealing with, was extremely helpful. The Emergency Room doctor had been fairly vague. The hand surgeon's details helped me stay calm for her.

- As we moved from the hospital to occupational therapist, my daughter's hand therapists treated much more than her hand; **they were amazing in helping her understand her new normal.**

Kindness, Gentleness, Specifics and Staying Calm truly enhanced our patient experience.

The Courage to Bend Some Rules

In 1992, I spent a week in the Intensive Care Unit. As a member of the Notre Dame swim team, we were in an accident that left two of my teammates dead and many of us with various injuries. I had broken my back, had two emergency surgeries, and was paralyzed.

During the first 48 hours I was in ICU, I had over 100 people visit me. In ICU! That never happens. For many reasons (all of them valid), it's not supposed to happen. There are rules and regulations in place to keep all patients safe, as there should be.

But I was 18 years old and, unlike many of the other patients, I was conscious. We were all young and we were all hurting, both physically and emotionally. And all my teammates needed to see me. And I needed to see all my teammates. So one by one, they came to visit me (often times with their own parents who had come to check on their child). And when I was resting or being attended to by the staff, they waited until I was awake and free to see visitors. For 48 hours, it was a non-stop parade of teammates, family, and friends.

Was this routine policy? No. But it set the tone for my care during my two-month hospital stay. It comforted the fears of a young girl who was scared she would never walk again. It kept me connected to my college family which made all the difference in my emotional (and therefore physical) recovery as I set out on a wild journey.

Whenever possible, if it's safe to bend the rules please have the courage to try!

"Healing is an art. It takes time, it takes practice, it takes love."

— Anonymous

"Treat the patient as a whole, not just the hole in the patient."

— Dr. John Macdonald

Advice from a Professional Patient

By Swapna Kakani

The scars from 65 surgeries in my 30 years have taught me simple truths.

1. **Meet Patients Where They Are:** At the age of 10, I was sitting in the endocrinologist outpatient clinic. He was just one of the many specialists I had to see regularly. It was my first time to see him. He did something I have only had one doctor do since. He walked in, sat on the exam table, put my chart next to him, and leaned toward me, with his eyes just on me, not on my dad sitting next to me. The endocrinologist said, "What is your goal, what do you want to get out of this, and how can I help you get there." Unfortunately, I did not have an answer. I was 10. I was shocked though. He cared. I heard in a talk once, "Patients don't care what you know until they know you care." It is so true. By his simple actions and dialogue, I knew he cared. This doctor **wanted to meet me where I was.** He wanted to know my goal even if I was 10 years old. He knew this was not the one and only time I was going to see him. This is a chronic disease. This is a chronic relationship. He was willing to empower me.

2. **We cannot assume in healthcare.** My pediatric GI told parents "You are lucky your child is alive." "You should be happy your child is alive. Period." Of course, I am grateful to be alive, but that is not the whole story. We cannot assume that is the only desired goal. I need a team that respects what it takes for me to live! My goal is to LIVE not to SURVIVE. Now we beg to survive in crisis mode and the best clinicians are trained to get patients out of crisis modes. But what about life after crisis mode. The life we live to prevent crises, the decisions we make to live and cope with disease do not necessarily cure it. I see clinical care providers struggle to appreciate; they understand and often assume, but to appreciate takes compassion from the heart not the brain. It is important to have the ability to *not* assume, but instead to know what chronic disease life looks like, feels like, for *me*.

3. **Every patient has a story that adds value to their care, it is up to us to listen to it:** It takes honest conversations between providers and chronic disease patients where both have respected where the other is coming from. To appreciate one another's etiology, knowledge, experience, and engagement – simply to know one another. That can be more powerful than a protocol, a data point, or a metric. Patient stories and life experiences can sometimes dictate care over what always has been done. Ask patients what they care about. Knowing their goals and why they have those

goals can change patient care. Value patients beyond their label as patients.

4. **My provider needs to be curious:** It was 2011, and my Dad and I were sitting alone with the surgeon in a treatment room at the local hospital. The surgeon had just finished digging into my skin with his scalpel, purposefully making a small fistula bigger. We were stuck, I had a sequence of 13 abdominal surgeries in the last 4 months due to a constant sequence of complications, which left me with fistulas that showed no sign of healing. The pediatric surgeon wanted another doctor on board. His only question to our recommendations was, "Are they curious?" At the time curiosity signified passion, commitment, and thinking outside the box. My case was and is complicated, any medical professional who came on board had to be curious because my journey would not be simple. But, since the day the term "curious" has been coined, it has become to mean more. It has become to define my standards in a Doctor. Passion, commitment, outside of the box thinking, but more importantly do they see me as an equal member of the medical team, do they know my personality, my good & bad habits, my goals, and lifelong dreams?

5. **It is ok to say sorry:** In 30 years, I have only had one physician say sorry to me. Apology when warranted is needed and appreciated by patients.

It keeps providers accountable and makes them look human. Empathy and compassion, not sympathy, is important at the bedside. In 2010, I had an abdominal surgery that resulted in surgical complications and required 2 additional emergency abdominal surgeries within 2 weeks from the first surgery. I longed for a provider to take an extra minute during rounds or in their daily schedule to listen to my pain, my fears, my frustration of having complications, and say I am sorry for what has happened, let us talk about how we are going to handle it and move forward from here.

Warmth

Your fancy lobbies are attractive but sometimes overwhelming.

The artwork on the walls helps distract us from what's really going on.

The cafeteria is an oasis in a confusing place.

The band on my wrist makes me feel secure but also weird.

No matter what the medical journey is... tests, surgery, emergencies,

We are seeking the best decisions for the best outcome and,

We're desperately seeking warmth along the way.

The warmth in your eyes while you find out who we are and when you must tell us an unexpected result.

The warmth of a blanket while trying to rest and calm down.

The warmth of a washcloth placed with care on our brow.

How you take the time to warm the equipment before you place it on me.

The warmth of a hug when you see we need one.

The coldness of these intimidating experiences is unavoidable.

Please remember warmth can make all the difference in the world!

Be Aware and Beware

Yes, we knew that you have years of training to know what he needed before and after surgery.

Our son was anxious to get back to the field and we saw hope with the plan you developed.

He was ready for all the challenges explained and trusted the team with all aspects of his care.

When the post-surgery pain set in, he appreciated the medications and we trusted all the direction and prescriptions.

Instead of the minimum plan of pain attack, he was given a large number of pills to take home. He was also given an unimaginable new illness that took over all our lives.

We need caregivers to be aware that encouraging strength through the pain of healing is a short-term sacrifice and is much better than a life of potential addiction.

Your Bad Day is Our Bad Day

Through multiple hospital stays, we watched the doctors, nurses, physical therapists and aides offer efficient and knowledgeable care for our Mother. This stream of competence was important but didn't stand out as we reflected on the overall care experience.

Unfortunately, the times that were more memorable were the days when caregivers were having a bad day. There were situations where questions were dismissed, conversations were rushed and even one moment when we were scolded for trying to assist when the call bell wasn't answered. We heard some half-hearted apologies and lots of excuses about being short-staffed, budget cuts and concerns about colleagues who don't pull their weight. We didn't need to know your concerns about your work conditions since we had enough concerns trying to recover in a strange place.

We know you're at your job while we're compromised in a hospital bed. We know not every day will be a good day for you. Our advice is that you understand your bad day becomes our bad day and just by being in the hospital, we're already having a not so good day.

Please remember it's difficult for us to handle the stresses of your job while we are in your care.

Shots

by Seth Hopkins, age 9

They make me scared because I know it's going to hurt.

It would be nice if you could give me a toy that I could play with to forget what you are going to do to me.

Now that I'm older I'd rather get a shot with my friends and not my mom.

Shots basically fill you with fear since you realize you're going to get pain even though it's quick it's very scary.

Thank you for making me healthy so I don't have diseases. Please next time be more careful because I'm scared. Kids love stickers and candy.

"The doctor should support the hope of the patient to recover."

— Hippocrates

"It can be argued that the largest yet most neglected resource, worldwide, is the patient."

— Warner Slack

Advice FOR the Patient

Preparing to be the Best Patient

O f course, we can't always pick our caregivers, especially when we're rushed to an emergency room. Despite not being able to pick and choose the best caregivers for our specific needs and desires in every location, every shift, every day, we can be diligent about participating effectively with our caregivers. Whether you are the patient or standing by a loved one receiving medical care, here's some *Advice FOR the Patient*:

1- Don't hesitate to speak up. If something is confusing or seems not to be in line with previous medical advice, ask questions, and keep asking questions until you feel your specific condition has been addressed.

2- If you have hearing or vision restrictions, be sure all caregivers are aware of it. Don't assume that everyone is aware.

3- Never hesitate to ask for assistance if you feel weak or unsteady. A fall can result in significant issues or death. Also, never lean on furniture or equipment that has wheels at home or in the hospital.

4- If your child is receiving emergency care, be sure to inquire whether the emergency room or urgent care center has pediatric-sized supplies.

5- Don't rush through medical history or other forms that you are asked to complete in a doctor's office or hospital. Your caregivers need all pieces of your puzzle to offer the best clinical decision-making.

6- Always share the names of all medications or other supplements you are taking. This is another crucial piece of your health puzzle. Also be clear about any allergies or food sensitivities you have.

7- Don't be shy about reminding staff about hand washing if you see a caregiver prepare to work with you without washing their hands. Infection control is one of the most important issues while you are in a hospital or outpatient setting. Don't be shy about having your visitors wash their hands and to assist you by wiping down your bedside table, bedrails etc. with anti-bacterial wipes.

8- If you have pain, say so. Pain can be an indication of infection or other issues that need attention. Your caregivers need your prompt reporting to get to the root cause of pain. Also, to avoid issues with opioid dependency, be aware that some levels of temporary pain may be better than extra pills.

9- If you are concerned about the transition back home and how well you will adjust, ask to speak with discharge planners who can offer many resources to make sure you are well prepared.

10- If people you've never seen enter your room, be sure to ask for identification and to understand their credentials.

We wish you well!
Diane and Haley

The Universal Patient Compact ™

W ays patients and caregivers can partner for exceptional care:

The Universal Patient Compact ™
Principles for Partnership

Universal Patient Compact Copyright © 2008 by the National Patient Safety Foundation. Used by permission of the Institute for Healthcare Improvement, ihi.org.

As a patient I pledge to:

- Be a responsible and active member of my health-care team
- Treat you with respect, honesty and consideration
- Always tell you the truth
- Respect the commitment you have made to healthcare and healing
- Give you the information that you need to treat me
- Learn all that I can about my condition
- Participate in decisions about my care
- Understand my care plan to the best of my ability
- Tell you what medications I am taking
- Ask questions when I do not understand and until I do understand
- Communicate any problems I have with the plan for my care
- Tell you if something about my health changes
- Tell you if I have trouble reading
- Let you know if I have family, friends or an advocate to help me with my healthcare

As your healthcare partner we (caregivers) pledge to:

- Include you as a member of the team
- Treat you with respect, honesty and compassion
- Always tell you the truth
- Include your family or advocate when you would like us to
- Hold ourselves to the highest quality and safety standards
- Be responsive and timely with our care and information to you
- Help you to set goals for your healthcare and treatment plans
- Listen to you and answer your questions
- Provide information to you in a way you can understand
- Respect your right to your own medical information
- Respect your privacy and the privacy of your medical information
- Communicate openly about benefits and risks associated with any treatments
- Provide you with the information to help you make informed decisions about your care and treatment options
- Work with you, and other partners who treat you, in the coordination of your care

"To know even one life has breathed easier because you have lived. This is to have succeeded."

— Ralph Waldo Emerson

The Authors/Editors

Haley Scott DeMaria is a patient advocate, author, and speaker. Her book, *What Though the Odds,* chronicles her dramatic recovery after suffering a serious back injury. As a freshman swimmer at the University of Notre Dame, Haley was left paralyzed when the team bus overturned in a snowstorm. The accident caused the death of two of her Fighting Irish teammates, while Haley's condition led to years of surgeries and rehabilitation. Her miraculous recovery has allowed her to live a full life, returning to walking, swimming, and even hiking Mount Kilimanjaro. Haley and her husband, Jamie, are the proud parents of James and Edward.

Diane S. Hopkins was one of the first Chief Experience Officers in the healthcare industry. She has extensive experience as a thought leader in the industry in the areas of innovation culture, marketing strategy and customer experience strategy. She is author of the book, *Unleashing the Chief Moment Officers* and co-author of the book, *Wake Up and Smell the Innovation*. She works with a variety of healthcare and non-healthcare companies as a content expert and consultant to improve customer experience and innovation strategy. She is a certified Experience Economy Expert and has been a frequent speaker at industry conferences including the Cleveland Clinic Empathy and Innovation conference. She was a founding faculty member at the University of Notre Dame IVIA Innovation mentor program, guest faculty at the Pennsylvania College of Health Science and committee member at the Patient Safety Movement. Also, she's the proud mother of Benjamin.

CPSIA information can be obtained
at www.ICGtesting.com
Printed in the USA
BVHW041017270120
570495BV00005BA/10

9 781647 040055